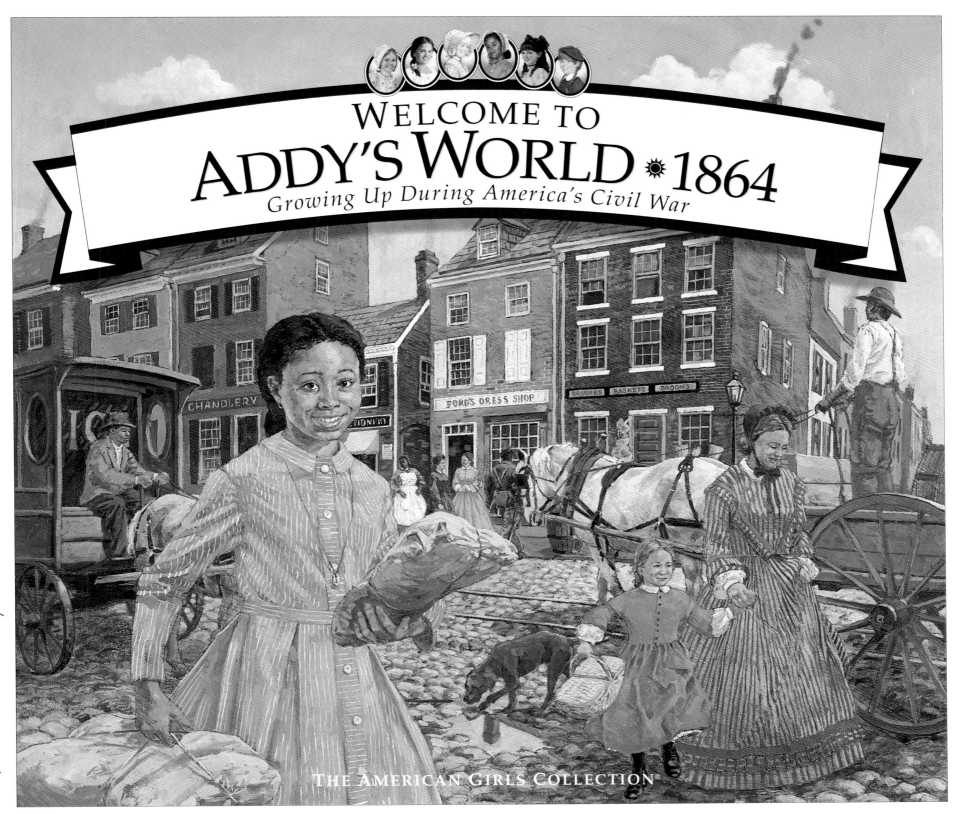

WELCOME TO
ADDY'S WORLD ☀ 1864
Growing Up During America's Civil War

CHANDLERY

FORD'S DRESS SHOP

BRUSHES BASKETS BROOMS

THE AMERICAN GIRLS COLLECTION®

American Girl™

Printed in Singapore
99 00 01 02 03 04 05 TWP 10 9 8 7 6 5 4 3 2
The American Girls Collection®, Addy®, Addy Walker®, and the
American Girl logo are trademarks of Pleasant Company.

Written by Susan Sinnott
Edited by Tamara England and Jodi Evert
Historical and Editorial Consulting by American Historical Publications
Designed and Art Directed by Mengwan Lin and Jane S. Varda
Produced by Lori Armstrong, Cheryll Mellenthin, and Paula Moon
Cover Illustration by Dahl Taylor
Interior Illustrations by Laszlo Kubinyi, Susan McAliley, Susan Moore, and Dahl Taylor
Illustrations Research by Rebecca Sample Bernstein
Photography by Jamie Young and Connie Russell
Prop Research and Styling by Jean doPico

Library of Congress Cataloging-in-Publication Data
Welcome to Addy's world, 1864 — growing up during America's Civil War /
[written by Susan Sinnott ; edited by Tamara England and Jodi Evert ;
designed by Mengwan Lin and Jane S. Varda ;
photography by Jamie Young and Connie Russell].
p. cm.—(The American girls collection)
Summary: Describes the conditions of African Americans in the
North and the South during and immediately after the Civil War.
ISBN 1-56247-771-4
1. United States—History—Civil War, 1861–1865—Social aspects—Juvenile literature.
2. United States—History—Civil War, 1861–1865—Afro-Americans—Juvenile literature.
3. Afro-American girls—Pennsylvania—Philadelphia—
Social life and customs—19th century—Juvenile literature.
4. Philadelphia (Pa.)—History—Civil War, 1861–1865—Social aspects—Juvenile literature
[1. United States—History—Civil War, 1861–1865.
2. Afro-Americans—History. 3. Slavery. 4. Race relations.]
I. Sinnott, Susan, 1952–   II. Kubinyi, Laszlo, 1937–   ill. III. Title. IV. Series.
E468.9.S583 1999 973.7'1—dc21

Table of Contents

Welcome to Addy's World

Addy kissed Esther and stroked her head.
"Don't worry, Esther. We coming back for you," she
whispered softly as she handed her rag doll to the baby.
"You hold on to Janie until I see you again."

—Meet Addy

In 1864, whispers of freedom spread through slave cabins all across the South. Parents like Addy's whispered plans for freedom deep into the night. Taking their families to freedom was risky, but many felt staying enslaved was worse. They could no longer stand to see their family members beaten and sold away.

In the fields, the music of freedom was everywhere. Slaves sang spirituals that had double meanings. When a slave owner heard "I Am Bound for the Promised Land," he thought the promised land was heaven. But to enslaved people, those words meant freedom in the North. At night in the slave quarters, steady drumbeats and soft singing often covered the footfalls of escaping slaves, urging them to run faster, run farther, to freedom.

"Freedom's got its cost," Uncle Solomon said to Addy as he handed her a half dime the night she and Momma fled the plantation. When Momma took hold of her hand that night and led her into the woods, Addy realized Uncle Solomon wasn't just talking about money. She looked back for a last glimpse of her baby sister, but her eyes were blurred with tears. Freedom had cost Addy her family and the only home she'd ever known.

Half dime

Just as Addy's family was split apart by slavery, the nation was split in two by the most terrible war in its history.

A Nation Divided

When Addy and Momma made their daring escape to freedom, America was in its third year of fighting the Civil War. The war started in 1861, when the country, or *Union*, divided—South against North. What differences were so great that they could split the nation in two?

THE SOUTH
Since the 1700s, the South had made most of its money from tobacco, rice, and cotton. These crops were in great demand in the North and in Europe. Slave labor made growing these crops fairly cheap, so southern plantation owners enjoyed large profits, and many grew wealthy.

THE NORTH
Slavery had been outlawed in the North since the early 1800s. The North didn't need slavery for its smaller farms and big-city businesses and factories. Most Northerners had never seen slavery up close. Many felt slavery was wrong, but as long as it stayed in the South, they let it be.

Slaves were sometimes shackled to keep them from running away.

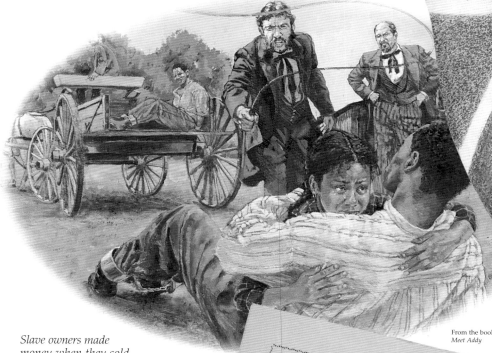

From the book Meet Addy

Slave owners made money when they sold their slaves. Most owners didn't care that a sale might separate a family.

FAMILIES TORN APART
This owner sold his slaves when he moved to Europe. Slaves were sold to the highest bidder and often never saw their families again.

HEWLETT & BRIGHT
BY
SALE OF
VALUABLE
SLAVES
(On account of departure)

The Owner of the following named and valuable Slaves, being on the eve of departure for Europe, will cause the same to be offered for sale, at the NEW EXCHANGE, corner of St. Louis and Chartres streets, on Saturday, May 16, at Twelve o'Clock, viz.

1. SARAH, a mulatress, aged 45 years, a good cook and accustomed to house work in general, is an excellent and faithful nurse for sick persons, and in every respect a first rate character.

2. DENNIS, her son, a mulatto, aged 24 years, a first rate cook and steward for a vessel, having been in that capacity for many years on board one of the Mobile packets; is strict, honest, temperate and a first rate subject.

3. CHOLE, a mulatress, aged 36 years, she is, without exception, one of the most competent servants in the country, a first rate washer and ironer, does up lace, a good cook and house-keeper; she would be invaluable to any person.

4. FANNY, her daughter, a mulatress, aged 16 years, speaks French and English, is a superior hairdresser, (pupil of Guillac,) a good seamstress and ladies' maid, is smart, intelligent, and a first rate character.

5. DANDRIDGE, a mulatto, aged 26 years, a first rate dining-room servant, a good painter and rough carpenter.

6. NANCY, a mulatto...

Rallying the Union

Southerners feared that the new president, Abraham Lincoln, would end slavery. Soon after the 1860 election, southern states began *seceding*, or separating, from the Union to form their own country—the *Confederate States of America*.

More than anything, Lincoln wanted to reunite America. He believed the five "border states"(shown in red) were the key to this goal. These states supported the Union, but they also wanted to keep slavery legal.

Lincoln believed slavery was wrong, but he knew the border states would secede if he declared a war to end slavery. His only hope was to rally the Union around one idea—defeating the South to reunite the nation. If he could do that, slavery just might end, too.

The U.S. Capitol in Washington

TURNING POINTS
In 1852, Harriet Beecher Stowe's book *Uncle Tom's Cabin* described just how evil slavery was. It appeared only two years after an important law gave slave owners the right to hunt runaways in the North. Northerners saw the cruelty of slavery up close and vowed to stop it.

THE SPLIT
Since the early 1800s, western territories were becoming part of the Union. Southerners wanted them to become slave states. Northerners did not. By the early 1860s, such differences led to talk of war.

The Nation at War

The first full battle of the war took place on a muggy Sunday in July 1861, just outside the town of Manassas, Virginia.

Many people from Washington thought it was a perfect day for a buggy ride to the countryside for a close-up look at the war. They were certain that the Union troops— the Yankees—would overwhelm the ragtag Confederate Rebels and that the war would come to a speedy end that very day.

They filled picnic hampers with fine food and wine and left for a day in the country. The ladies carried parasols to shield their delicate skin from the hot sun. The men, including senators and congressmen, brought binoculars for better viewing. As wave upon wave of Yankee soldiers in blue uniforms marched across an open field, women and children waved their hankies, threw flowers, and laughed and cheered.

Their smiles vanished quickly when the real fighting began. The air became a swirl of smoke and dust. Soldiers fell to the ground. Carts overturned as horses ran off in confusion. The smell of death hung in the air as heavy as the cannon smoke.

The Washington picnickers fled in panic, leaving champagne glasses and hampers behind. The fighting came so close that many of the spectators leaped into strangers' carriages and ordered the drivers to speed east. Others ran so fast they didn't even try to find a bridge across nearby Bull Run Creek. Instead, they plunged into the swiftly moving waters, where several drowned.

"We found . . . along the road parasols and dainty shawls lost in their fright by the frail, fair ones who had seats in most of the carriages," wrote a Confederate colonel.

When the first battle of Bull Run—also called the Battle of Manassas—was over, the Union troops had been badly beaten. There was no triumphant march to Richmond, Virginia, to close down the Confederate capital, as many had expected. Instead, the humiliated Yankee soldiers went back to Washington in disgrace. There they asked themselves what had gone wrong—and prepared for a much longer war than anyone had thought possible.

Four Long Years

Most people thought the war would last only a few months—at the most. Both Union and Confederate soldiers rushed to sign up. "We were all afraid it would be over and we not in the fight," said a 21-year-old Confederate soldier. They had no idea that the fighting would rage for four long years and cost more lives than all other American wars—both before and since—combined.

① BLOCKADE
As soon as the war started, Lincoln ordered the Union navy to block all southern ports. He wanted to stop southern ships from sailing to Europe to sell cotton and tobacco for cash and weapons to fight the North.

② REBELS
Southern soldiers were called *Rebels* because they *rebelled*, or fought against the Union. Enslaved people were not allowed to fight in the Rebel army, but their masters could take them along as servants.

③ HARD TIMES IN THE SOUTH
The war raged through the South, ruining cities, plantations, and small farms. As men left for war and more and more slaves ran away to freedom, southern women struggled to grow crops and feed their children.

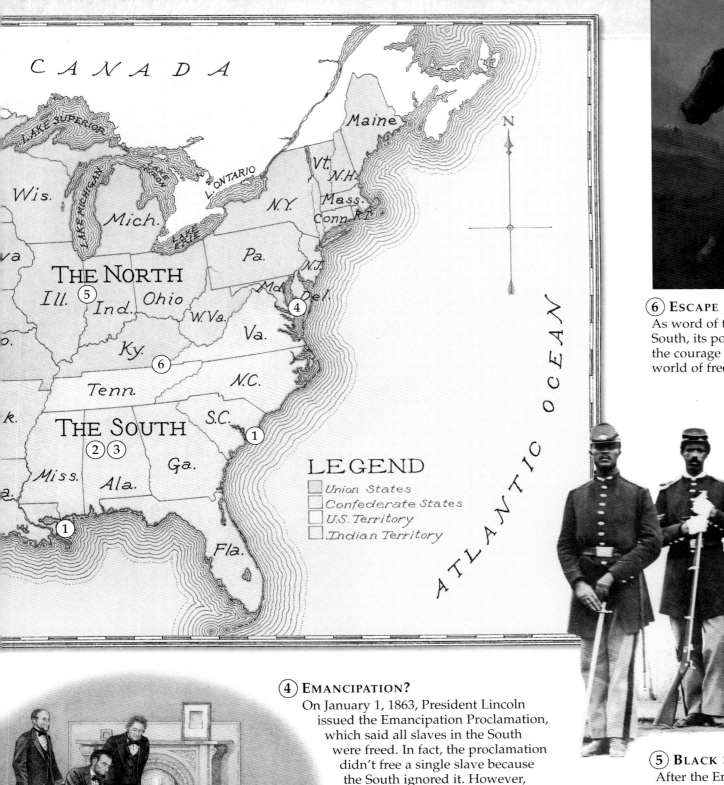

LEGEND
- Union States
- Confederate States
- U.S. Territory
- Indian Territory

6 ESCAPE
As word of the Emancipation Proclamation reached the South, its powerful message gave many enslaved people the courage to make the dangerous escape to a new world of freedom in the North.

5 BLACK SOLDIERS
After the Emancipation Proclamation, the Union army allowed black men to form their own *regiments*, or organized military groups, to fight for the North. One senator from Georgia wrote, *"If slaves seem good soldiers, then our whole theory of slavery is wrong."*

4 EMANCIPATION?
On January 1, 1863, President Lincoln issued the Emancipation Proclamation, which said all slaves in the South were freed. In fact, the proclamation didn't free a single slave because the South ignored it. However, there was great power in Lincoln's words. If the Union won the war, slavery would end in the South.

The Promise of the City

From the book *Addy Learns a Lesson*

Addy and Momma started a new life in freedom in Philadelphia.

As Addy and her mother stood on a busy pier in Philadelphia, they wondered if this big, strange city could ever be home to them. Was there room for even two more people in this crowded place? This was where freedom was, Poppa had said. And Addy wanted so much to believe him.

This was where the Declaration of Independence was signed in 1776, stating that *"all men are created equal."* Black people had never been equal to white people in the South. Would Addy and Momma find equality *and* freedom here in Philadelphia?

MAKING A HOME
In 1864, thousands of black people, both wealthy and poor, made Philadelphia their home. They had their own schools, churches, and businesses, and helped newcomers like Addy and her mother find homes and jobs.

THE LIBERTY BELL
Abolitionists, or people who spoke out against slavery, took part of the Liberty Bell's inscription for their motto: *"Proclaim liberty throughout the land."*

The ringing of the Liberty Bell called the people of Philadelphia to hear the first reading of the Declaration of Independence in 1776.

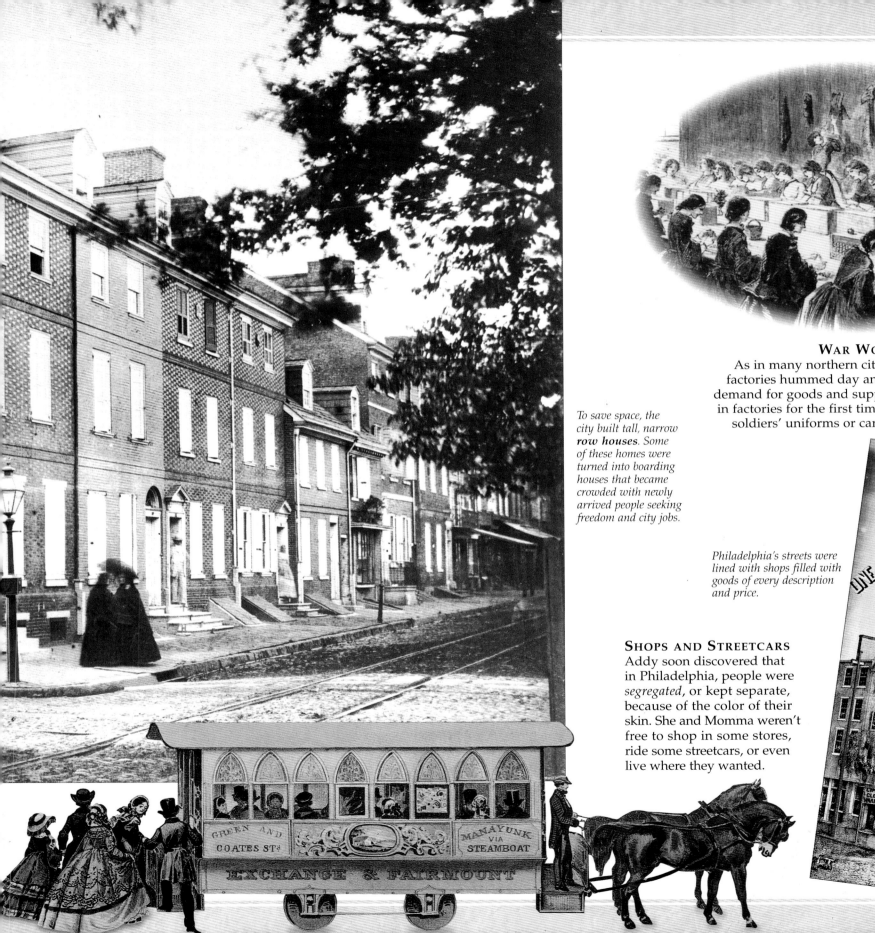

*To save space, the city built tall, narrow **row houses**. Some of these homes were turned into boarding houses that became crowded with newly arrived people seeking freedom and city jobs.*

WAR WORK
As in many northern cities, Philadelphia's factories hummed day and night to meet the demand for goods and supplies. Women worked in factories for the first time, making things like soldiers' uniforms or cartridges for bullets.

Philadelphia's streets were lined with shops filled with goods of every description and price.

SHOPS AND STREETCARS
Addy soon discovered that in Philadelphia, people were *segregated*, or kept separate, because of the color of their skin. She and Momma weren't free to shop in some stores, ride some streetcars, or even live where they wanted.

9

A Home in the City

Addy's family found a home in one of Philadelphia's many boarding houses. In these houses, people from different backgrounds—recently freed black people like the Walkers and lifelong free blacks from the North—lived together. There were also boarding houses where white people lived, but whites and blacks rarely lived side by side.

LIGHTING
As evening fell, gaslights lit cobblestone streets outside, and candles and kerosene lamps glowed inside.

CROWDED—BUT TOGETHER
A family of six shared this room. A baby slept in the cradle, and her parents slept in the big bed. Two sisters shared the small bed, and an older brother slept on the floor.

This former soldier lost his leg in the war.

NEWS
After dinner, boarders gathered in the parlor to visit and exchange news. Those who knew how could read the news of the Civil War aloud to others.

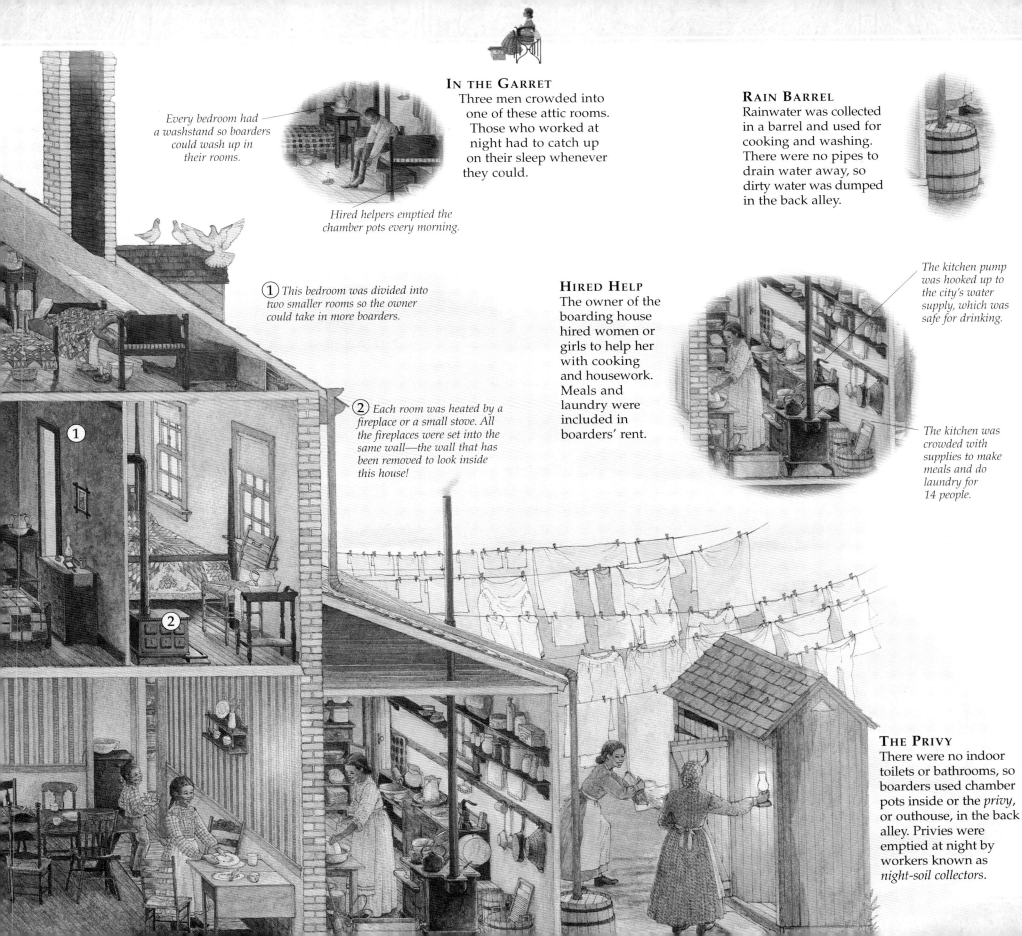

IN THE GARRET
Three men crowded into one of these attic rooms. Those who worked at night had to catch up on their sleep whenever they could.

Every bedroom had a washstand so boarders could wash up in their rooms.

Hired helpers emptied the chamber pots every morning.

RAIN BARREL
Rainwater was collected in a barrel and used for cooking and washing. There were no pipes to drain water away, so dirty water was dumped in the back alley.

① *This bedroom was divided into two smaller rooms so the owner could take in more boarders.*

② *Each room was heated by a fireplace or a small stove. All the fireplaces were set into the same wall—the wall that has been removed to look inside this house!*

HIRED HELP
The owner of the boarding house hired women or girls to help her with cooking and housework. Meals and laundry were included in boarders' rent.

The kitchen pump was hooked up to the city's water supply, which was safe for drinking.

The kitchen was crowded with supplies to make meals and do laundry for 14 people.

THE PRIVY
There were no indoor toilets or bathrooms, so boarders used chamber pots inside or the *privy*, or outhouse, in the back alley. Privies were emptied at night by workers known as *night-soil collectors*.

Fun and Games

Addy and Momma worked hard to build a new life in freedom, but there was still time for fun. Everyone—young and old alike—enjoyed the pleasures of visiting and storytelling. Girls like Addy and Sarah had fun jumping rope on Philadelphia's brick sidewalks. Boys played with marbles and balls. Addy's father carved handmade toys and games for Addy and Esther out of wood scraps. In Philadelphia's fine stores, toys made by machines were on display, but families like the Walkers couldn't afford fancy store-bought toys.

From the book Happy Birthday, Addy!

SPELLING BLOCKS
Spelling blocks helped children learn letters and practice making words. Machine-made blocks were sold in stores, but some families made and decorated them by hand.

GAMES
Children played The White Horse, a popular game from England, with cards and small disks.

MADE WITH LOVE
Handmade cloth dolls and animals carved from wood were some of the simple toys that children enjoyed in the 1860s.

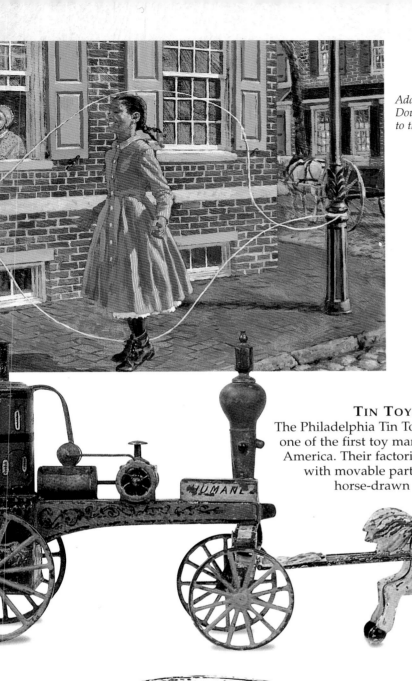

Addy learned to jump Double Dutch by listening to the rhythm of the ropes.

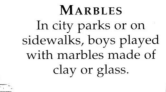

MARBLES
In city parks or on sidewalks, boys played with marbles made of clay or glass.

TIN TOYS
The Philadelphia Tin Toy Factory was one of the first toy manufacturers in America. Their factories made toys with movable parts like this horse-drawn cart.

MOVING PICTURES
The *zoetrope* (ZO-ee-trohp) is an optical-illusion toy. Children placed paper strips inside it that showed figures in motion and then spun the drum as they watched through the side slits. The figures seemed to come alive!

PUNCH!
This spring toy was known as a *punch-box* because its face was similar to a popular puppet named Punch.

Hard at Work

Addy's father was angry that many white shop owners wouldn't hire him as a carpenter. Why, he wondered, should his talent be wasted simply because of the color of his skin? Many black people asked themselves the same question. Some found the answer by starting their own businesses. Others found white employers who would give them a chance. Many simply took whatever jobs they could find. All blacks were paid less than whites for the same work. "It ain't fair," Addy protested. "No," Poppa answered, "But that's the way it is."

From the book Happy Birthday, Addy!

Poppa finally found a job as a carpenter in Philadelphia.

CATERERS
Many black *caterers*, or people hired to put on parties, got their start working in the kitchens of wealthy white people. Philadelphia's Thomas Dorsey escaped slavery and became a world-class caterer who prepared food for visiting royalty.

BARBERS
During the 1860s, the best barbershops were for white people only. A black man named William Warwich owned one of these shops, but he couldn't give his own brother a shave there. If he did, his high-paying white customers would stop coming.

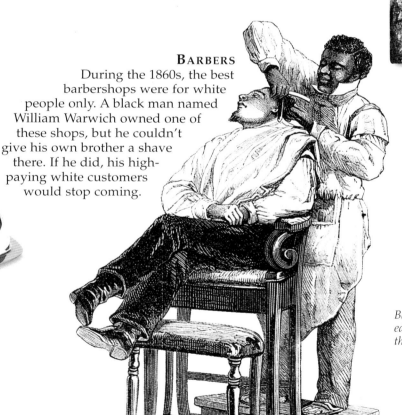

SERVING OTHERS
Butlers, coachmen, nannies, and personal maids were proud of their fine manners and crisp appearance. Many traveled to fashionable resorts with their employers and enjoyed handsome hand-me-down clothes.

Barbers used straight-edged razors to shave their customers.

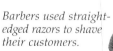

TEACHERS
In 1862, Mary Jane Patterson was one of the first African American women to graduate from Ohio's Oberlin College. After teaching for several years at Philadelphia's Institute for Colored Youth, she became the principal of a high school for black students in Washington.

GRAND
Complimentary Concert
TO
MADAME MARY L. BROWN,
On which occasion, the renowned Vocalist,
MISS E. T. GREENFIELD, the
BLACK SWAN,
Will appear, having in the kindest manner volunteered her highly valuable services. Also,
MR. S. MORGAN SMITH,
Who has kindly consented to sing for

PROFESSOR KENIG WILL PRES

Tickets, 25 Cents. Rese
To be had at the principal Mu
on the Com

Doors open at 7 o'clock.

The Piano used on this
Mr. J. E. Goul

ARTISTS
Black artists had to look hard for support, encouragement, and buyers for their work. David Bustill Bowser worked as a sign painter during the day and painted fine landscapes and portraits late at night.

THE BLACK SWAN
Elizabeth Taylor Greenfield was called "the Black Swan" because of the elegance of her voice and the grace of her stage presence. In 1854, she became the first African American singer to perform for Britain's royal family. But she never performed at Philadelphia's Academy of Music, which didn't allow blacks inside until 1877, a year after her death.

Some people made a living playing music on Philadelphia's streets.

Mrs. Lincoln's Dressmaker

While Addy's mother was hard at work as a seamstress in Philadelphia, another seamstress and former slave, Elizabeth Keckley, became one of the most successful dressmakers in Washington.

As a slave in St. Louis, Lizzie had been in great demand as a high-fashion seamstress and had sewn dresses for many of her owner's friends. Lizzie's owner was more generous than most and allowed Lizzie to keep the money she earned. Lizzie eventually raised $1,200—enough to buy her freedom from slavery.

VARINA DAVIS
In 1861, Varina Davis asked Lizzie to move with her to Richmond, Virginia, where her husband, Jefferson Davis, would become president of the Confederate States. Lizzie refused.

Hand-stitched trims of lace, ribbon, feathers, and flowers added an elegant finishing touch.

OPEN FOR BUSINESS
In 1860, Lizzie Keckley moved to Washington. She attracted so many loyal customers that she was able to open her own dressmaking business. She rented two rooms in a boarding house—one for her home and one for her workshop.

The fashionably wide dresses of the 1860s could take as many as 25 yards of material!

Lizzie's own dresses reflected elegant design details, such as set-in sleeves decorated with contrasting trim.

A good pair of scissors was a seamstress's most important tool.

MARY LINCOLN

Mary Todd Lincoln, wife of President Abraham Lincoln, loved beautiful clothes and wanted the most skilled of all seamstresses. She chose Lizzie, who later became Mrs. Lincoln's close friend as well as her dressmaker.

It was easier and faster to stitch wide skirts by machine, but the fine finish work was still done by hand.

FOLLOWING FASHION

Dressmakers like Lizzie Keckley looked at *Godey's Lady's Book*, the most popular fashion magazine, for design ideas.

Civil War sewing box

Lizzie sewed more than 60 bows and hundreds of small dots on this dress.

This sewing tool was both a tape measure and a pincushion.

Darning needle and thread

Fashion

Handsome trim and stylish buttons were fashionable details, even on everyday dresses.

Even in the middle of the Civil War, women followed fashion. Wealthy women—both black and white—relied on seamstresses like Lizzie Keckley to keep them looking up-to-date and elegant. To satisfy her customers, a seamstress had to do fine work, have an eye for detail, and know how to find fabrics and notions made scarce by the war.

Buttons were removed from worn-out dresses and sewn on new ones.

HOOPSKIRTS

Hoopskirts were so wide they made it difficult for women to pass one another on the sidewalk.

Corsets gave women stylishly small waists.

Hoops made of metal or whalebone gave skirts their fullness.

LADIES' HATS

Women "freshened" their hats by replacing the ribbon or trim.

RETICULE

Most dresses did not have pockets, so a woman might carry a *reticule* (REH-tih-kyool), a small drawstring pouch. This reticule is decorated with cantaloupe seeds!

GIRLS' FASHIONS
Young girls wore muslin or cotton dresses for everyday wear. Girls sometimes added aprons or pinafores to keep their dresses clean longer.

This toddler's dress followed the fashions of the day—a wide neckline, pretty pleats, and black trim on brightly colored fabric.

DRESSES FOR BOYS AND GIRLS
As this photo of a mother and her two sons shows, very young boys wore dresses. They switched to short pants when they were about five years old, and then to long trousers at age twelve.

A STYLISH STONE
When Prince Albert of England died in 1861, Queen Victoria wore mourning jewelry made of *black onyx* (AH-nix), a beautiful black quartz. Soon it became all the rage in America. *Jet* jewelry, made of polished coal, was less expensive but still stylish.

TIP-TOP TOES
Ribbons, beadwork, and fancy hand-stitching were important details— even on shoes!

19

Meet the Fortens

Philadelphia's black community included people who were very poor and others with great wealth, such as Charlotte Forten. Charlotte's grandfather James Forten started a sailmaking business in 1788 and soon was one of the wealthiest men in Philadelphia. James raised his children and grandchildren to use their wealth and influence to help others, especially other black people.

Charlotte did just that. After an education in Salem, Massachusetts, Charlotte went south to teach the children of former slaves. But frail health forced her to return to Philadelphia, where she was active in the anti-slavery movement. Her uncle, abolitionist Robert Purvis, and his family often stayed with Charlotte—and helped her host elegant dinner parties that drew together Philadelphia's abolitionist community.

① *Even elegant homes didn't have bathrooms. The chamber pots and washstands were emptied and cleaned by servants, whose rooms were in the garret.*

② *Pictures were hung from picture rails so that nails wouldn't damage the walls.*

③ *Most homes didn't have closets, so clothes were stored in large wooden wardrobes.*

WRITING DESK
Charlotte kept a daily journal in which she wrote about her life before, during, and after the Civil War.

GREAT BOOKS
Charlotte read great books and studied and wrote late most nights. Charlotte felt her journal would help her *"judge correctly of the growth and improvement of my mind from year to year."*

PARTY PREPARATIONS
Preparing and serving a large, formal meal with many courses required the help of many servants. Charlotte probably hired extra help when she hosted a dinner party.

④ *The staircase and side wall have been removed to look inside this house.*

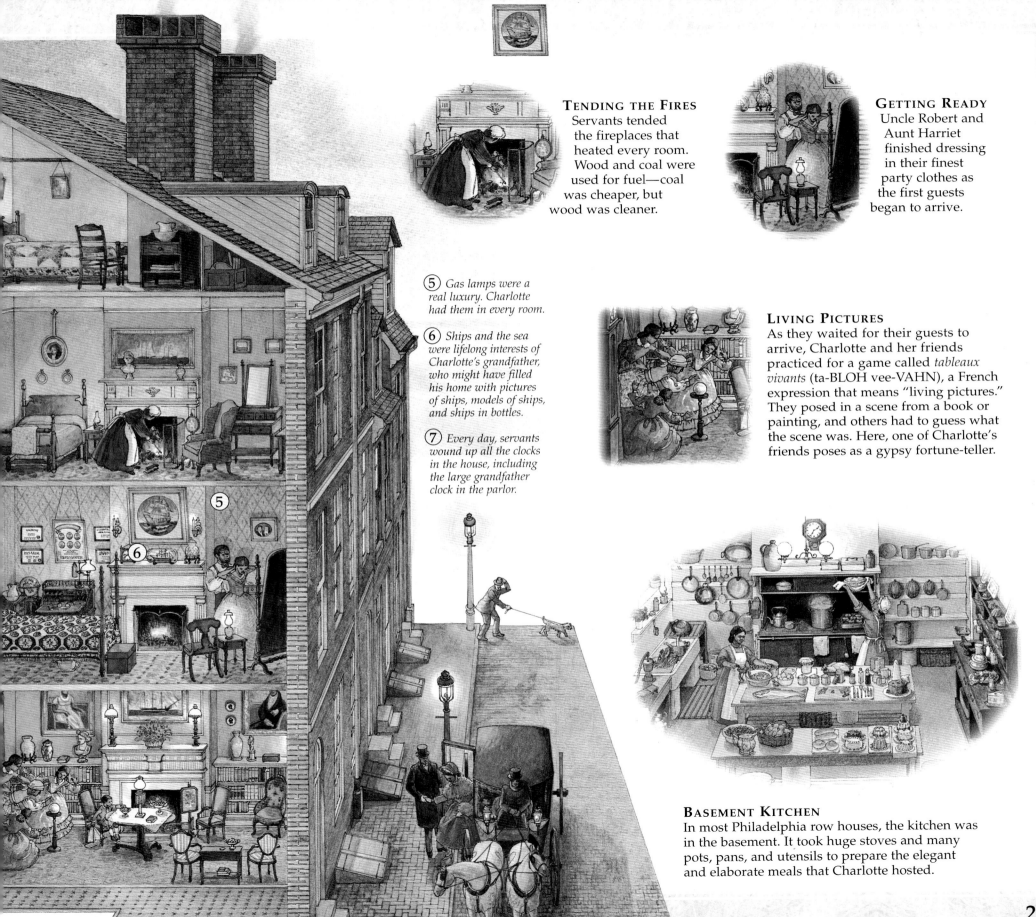

TENDING THE FIRES
Servants tended the fireplaces that heated every room. Wood and coal were used for fuel—coal was cheaper, but wood was cleaner.

GETTING READY
Uncle Robert and Aunt Harriet finished dressing in their finest party clothes as the first guests began to arrive.

(5) Gas lamps were a real luxury. Charlotte had them in every room.

(6) Ships and the sea were lifelong interests of Charlotte's grandfather, who might have filled his home with pictures of ships, models of ships, and ships in bottles.

(7) Every day, servants wound up all the clocks in the house, including the large grandfather clock in the parlor.

LIVING PICTURES
As they waited for their guests to arrive, Charlotte and her friends practiced for a game called *tableaux vivants* (ta-BLOH vee-VAHN), a French expression that means "living pictures." They posed in a scene from a book or painting, and others had to guess what the scene was. Here, one of Charlotte's friends poses as a gypsy fortune-teller.

BASEMENT KITCHEN
In most Philadelphia row houses, the kitchen was in the basement. It took huge stoves and many pots, pans, and utensils to prepare the elegant and elaborate meals that Charlotte hosted.

The Church

Churches held community fairs to raise money for families in need.

From the book *Addy Saves the Day*

When Addy and Momma arrived in Philadelphia, the church was there to help them. All-black churches had helped newcomers since 1794, when black leaders founded Mother Bethel Church to protest the way blacks were treated in white churches. In white churches, blacks were forced to sit quietly in separate sections far from the minister. In their own church, blacks could sit where they wished. Church-goers participated in services that were filled with music. By the time Addy arrived in Philadelphia, the city's many black churches formed the center of black social and religious life.

PRECIOUS BELONGINGS
Bibles and hymnals were treasured symbols of faith. Many families recorded births, marriages, and deaths in their Bibles.

Girls embroidered or cross-stitched bookmarks to mark their favorite biblical passages or hymns.

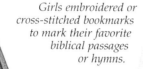

MOTHER BETHEL CHURCH
Mother Bethel African Methodist Episcopal Church was the country's first black-only religious *denomination*, or organization.

PEACE BE WITHIN THY WALLS

Men and women sat in separate sections in Mother Bethel Church.

MINISTERS

Ministers were highly respected leaders in northern black communities. Some were simply street preachers who had little education but could attract loyal followers. Others, like Alexander Crummell, were well educated. Reverend Crummell was educated at Cambridge University in England.

The Quakers

The peace-loving Society of Friends, also called *Quakers*, is a religious group that opposed slavery and provided strong leadership in the anti-slavery movement. There were more than a thousand seats at the Friends Meeting House on Philadelphia's Arch Street, and most Sundays they were all filled.

The Quakers believed as strongly in education as they did in abolition. In 1837, the Quakers founded the Institute for Colored Youth, or I.C.Y., for black students ages 11 and up. The I.C.Y. was the first Philadelphia school to hire black teachers and principals. Its goal was to train African American students to become teachers, either in the South or elsewhere in the North. The I.C.Y. was a force in Philadelphia's black community. Its large library was available both to students and to the public, and it was a gathering place for the community. Important leaders of the day, such as abolitionist Frederick Douglass, often came to the I.C.Y. to speak out against slavery and to encourage black students to work hard and succeed.

The Institute for Colored Youth

A Man Saved

In the spring of 1859, a former slave named Daniel Webster Dangerfield was arrested at his farm near Harrisburg, Pennsylvania. After working and living there in freedom for nine years, Mr. Dangerfield was at risk. A southern slave owner had claimed that Daniel was one of his runaway slaves. He threatened to take Daniel back into slavery.

The 1850 Fugitive Slave Act allowed slave owners to do just that. It said that a slave owner could come into the northern states and capture people who used to be his "property." In the North, abolitionists and average citizens—white and black—fought this law by hiding escaped slaves, taking down "wanted" posters put up by slave hunters, and refusing to help anyone looking for runaways.

Charlotte Forten's uncle Robert Purvis went to Philadelphia's courthouse to plead for Daniel's release. Abolitionists from around the country, such as Frederick Douglass and Quaker Lucretia Mott, joined the fight. Still, there was little hope that Daniel would be released and given his freedom again.

Lucretia Mott

Blacks accused of being fugitive slaves were nearly always found guilty and returned to the South.

Daniel's trial lasted three long days. In the end, the commissioner announced an extraordinary decision. He ruled that the slave owner had identified the wrong man. Daniel Webster Dangerfield was saved!

Frederick Douglass

Two days later, Charlotte Forten and Robert Purvis attended an anti-slavery rally to celebrate the victory. A crowd of southern men, angered over Daniel winning his freedom, came determined to stir up trouble. *"They created a great disturbance, stamping, hallooing, groaning, etc., so that it was impossible to hear a word,"* wrote Charlotte in her journal. The angry Southerners rushed the podium. *"We thought we should be crushed,"* wrote Charlotte. The police were called, but few expected them to help. To everyone's surprise, the police arrested the southern demonstrators.

Charlotte Forten

The next evening, Charlotte invited Daniel to dine at her home. The outcome of his trial and the arrests at the rally had given her new hope. Perhaps attitudes were changing. She felt she was not so alone in demanding an end to slave holding and slave hunting.

Robert Purvis

The court had given Daniel his freedom, but he knew that wouldn't stop angry Southerners from taking the law into their own hands. They might try to capture him again, or even kill him. Daniel decided to leave his home and set off for Canada—*"the only true free soil nearby,"* Charlotte noted regretfully. Two weeks later, Charlotte reported, *"Daniel has left us, and we hear with joy that he is safe in Canada."*

Plantation Life

B y the middle of the Civil War, plantations throughout the South were in trouble. The success of plantations depended completely upon the work of enslaved people. When owners left to fight in the war, many of their slaves escaped to the North. Owners' wives, left on their own, struggled to raise their children and manage the plantations without enough help. The slaves who remained had even more backbreaking work to do. Crops gradually became smaller and plantations lost money. And, as the war raged through the South, many plantations were damaged by battles or raided by soldiers—both Rebel and Yankee—in need of food and supplies.

① THE BIG HOUSE

The owner's family lived in the "big house." With fewer house slaves to clean, sew, cook, and tend to the needs of the owner's family, many of these beautiful houses became run-down.

② KITCHEN

House slaves also worked inside the hot and smoky kitchen, or *cookhouse*, to prepare meals for the owner's family.

③ ④ SMOKEHOUSE AND CHICKEN COOP

Slaves preserved meats in the smokehouse and hunted for eggs around the chicken coop. Sometimes they had to guard these provisions from raiding soldiers!

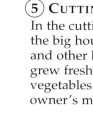

⑤ CUTTING GARDENS

In the cutting gardens near the big house, the cook and other house slaves grew fresh herbs and vegetables for the owner's meals.

⑥ ⑦ BARN AND CARRIAGE SHED

Slaves had always tended the plantation's horses, mules, and oxen and made sure carriages, harnesses, and plows were in good working order. But as the war continued, many animals were taken by soldiers.

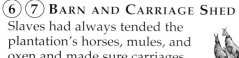

⑭ CEMETERIES
Most plantations had separate cemeteries for family members and slaves.

⑬ OVERSEER'S HOUSE
The overseer and his family lived in a cabin near the fields, where he could keep an eye on the slaves as they worked. But many overseers left to fight, too. The overseer's wife often helped the owner's wife manage the plantation.

⑫ COTTON PRESS
In spite of the war, the work of the plantation continued. Cotton was packed into *bales*, or bundles, on a press powered by a horse.

⑪ SOLD!
Owners desperate for money sold more of their slaves. But even this didn't bring in enough money to keep plantations running as they had before the war started.

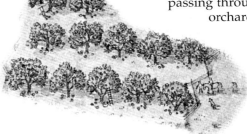

⑩ ORCHARDS
Many apple and peach trees went untended as more and more slaves escaped. Soldiers passing through often raided orchards for food.

⑧ SLAVE QUARTERS

Most slaves lived in small cabins away from the big house. The quarters were usually near a spring or a woods for a good supply of water and firewood.

⑨ SLAVE GARDENS
Slaves were allowed to have their own gardens. The corn, peas, and collard greens they grew added variety and nutrition to the food provided by the owner—which decreased as the war continued.

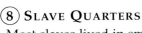

A Day's Work

Slaves didn't have clocks or calendars to mark the passage of time. Each day started and ended like the next—with hard work. Some slaves said that the workday lasted from "can't see to can't see" because they started work before sunrise and finished after dark. Hard work turned weeks into months and years. A year was made up of seed time, cotton blossom time, harvest, and Christmas. Years were recalled by events such as "the early frost," "the big storm," or "the master's death."

UP BEFORE DAWN
Just before dawn, the sound of a bell, horn, or conch shell called slaves to the fields. At the end of the workday, the same sound called them home again.

Hand-carved wooden work horn

TENDING TOBACCO
As tobacco plants grew, the top leaves had to be kept free of worms. One girl on a Virginia plantation remembered that if she missed a worm, she would have to "bite all de worms dat you miss . . . or git three lashes on you back."

Cotton bolls had to be picked by hand.

GOOD WORKING ORDER
Most slaves never saw a doctor. The plantation mistress used homemade remedies to keep slaves healthy so they could keep working. "When I'd be feeling poorly," said a former slave from Alabama, "my mistress did me up with castor oil, jimson root, and dogwood tea."

Owners and overseers usually kept a whip nearby to control and punish slaves who might try to escape.

THE COTTON GIN

The cotton gin *(jin)* was invented in 1793. It could remove seeds from cotton fifty times faster than a person could. As a result, owners planted even more cotton for slaves to tend.

CHILDREN'S WORK

Children as young as five could sweep, kindle fires, herd cattle, and start picking cotton. By the time boys and girls were teenagers, they did the work of adults.

MIDDAY MUSH

A slave's noonday meal was usually little more than a pot of cornmeal mush. Those who were quickest ate the most. On some plantations, slaves had plenty of food, but on others, there was never quite enough to satisfy everyone's hunger.

At the end of the day, slaves carried cotton from the field.

Senna leaves aided digestion. Hawthorn berries helped soothe sore throats.

Ginseng root was used to cure headaches and upset stomachs.

Children sometimes used oyster shells to scoop up mush.

Family Bonds

Strong and loving bonds among family members and friends helped make life bearable in spite of the hardships of slavery. It was against the law for slaves to marry, but many masters and slaves viewed couples as husband and wife and their children as members of one family—as long as they were together on the plantation. But when there was money to be made from selling slaves, owners would separate families without hesitation. And as Addy and her family knew, the pain of separation was almost too deep to bear.

Four generations of an enslaved family in 1862

Jumping the Broom
Marriages took place without papers and with little ceremony. Sometimes the master read the vows. "They says to de girl, 'You loves dis man?'" remembered a North Carolina woman, "Dey says to de man, 'You loves dis girl?' . . . If you say yes, dey brings in de broom and holds it 'bout a foot off de floor and say to you to jump over. Den he says you's married."

Motherhood
New mothers quickly returned to work in the fields or the big house. Field slaves often brought their new babies with them, laid them on quilts in the shade, and fed them during breaks.

MAKING TIME FOR PLAY

Many parents found ways to make simple dolls and toys for their children. And children found time to run and jump just for the joy of it. They jumped rope, rode stick horses, and played ball, marbles, or hiding games. Children of house slaves often played with the master's children—at least for a while.

We loved each other like brothers and sisters...but when the young masters and misses get older, they sent away from home to school. When they return...the whip is put in their hands.
a former slave

Young girls often took care of toddlers.

The Auction Block

The greatest threat to family life came from the auction block, where slaves were sold to the highest bidder. Cotton plantations in the Deep South needed a lot of slaves, and owners were willing to pay high prices. One witness to a sale of slaves wrote: *"I have seen 100 cases where families were separated. I have seen them in droves, 150 or 200 together—men, women, and children—linked side by side. I have seen children from eight or nine years old . . . and when the mothers were sold, heard them cry fit to break their hearts."*

Enslaved people were considered property that could be won in a raffle, just like horses.

Slaves were often chained or shackled when taken to auction.

Religion

Religion helped some enslaved people endure the cruelties of daily life and hold on to the hope of a better future. Some slave owners encouraged their slaves to be religious because they believed Christianity taught obedience. But to make sure that only the "right" values were passed along, slaves were not permitted to hold church services without a white person present.

LESSONS

Some plantation masters gathered the youngest slave children and read Bible stories that stressed discipline and obedience. "'Church' was what they called it," remembered one woman, "but the point was always 'how to be a good slave.'"

BIBLE QUILT

Slaves were not allowed to learn to read—not even the Bible. But quilts such as this one, sewn with scenes from the Bible, helped them remember and share religious stories.

PRAYER MEETINGS

Many slaves secretly held their own prayer meetings. Out of the master's sight and hearing, they sang and prayed as loudly as they wanted. A North Carolina woman remembered, "My mother she sing and pray to the Lord to deliver us out of slavery."

① **ADAM AND EVE**
The figures of Adam and Eve—and the serpent!—are shown in the Garden of Eden.

FUNERALS

When a slave died, the closest relative would ask the master for permission to sit up all night to sing and pray next to the dead person's body. Later, the mourners walked to the slave cemetery, where they marched around the grave to a steady drumbeat and shouted out their grief.

⑤ AFRICAN ANIMALS

The elephants may be remembered—or imagined—from tales told of life in Africa.

④ THE BIRTH OF JESUS

In this square, angels announce to shepherds in the fields the birth of the baby Jesus.

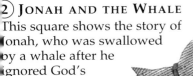

② JONAH AND THE WHALE

This square shows the story of Jonah, who was swallowed by a whale after he ignored God's wishes.

③ NOAH'S ARK

Several quilt squares show pairs of animals that Noah brought onto his ark to protect them from the flood.

Links to Africa

When Africans were brought against their will to America, they were torn away from everything they held most dear. Slave owners separated them from family and friends and forbade their customs and languages—everything that made them African. Most black people arrived from Africa with little more than the things they were wearing when they were captured, such as necklaces, rings, bracelets, or decorated belts. These items became cherished reminders of their African past and were handed down to children and grandchildren.

BUILDING STYLES
Slaves often used African building styles, such as this round fence, in the slave quarters.

Enslaved people wove American grasses, pine needles, and other materials into African-style baskets.

JEWELRY
Women combined animal teeth, bones, shells, seeds, and beads into beautiful necklaces, just as they had in Africa.

Eye

Eye beads and blue beads were thought to have powers that would protect the wearer from "the evil eye."

Knucklebones made into beads were thought to carry the strength and spirit of the dead person whose knuckles were used.

The People Had Wings

A master could take away his slaves' freedom, but he couldn't take away the power of their imagination. As evening settled on the slave quarters, young and old alike gathered in cabins or under the stars to share jokes, riddles, songs, and stories. Children sat spellbound as adults spun tales that mixed their African past with their life in America. One of the most powerful of these tales was called "The People Had Wings."

Long ago in Africa, the story begins, some of the people had magic inside them. They could grow beautiful wings and fly like birds.

Then white men captured some of these people and put them on a boat. The people had to leave their beautiful wings behind. There was no room for them on the boat. The crowded boat rocked and rolled with the sea, making the people miserable and sick.

When they reached America and were sold into slavery, their hearts grew sick, too. They forgot all about flying. But the magic was still inside them.

One of these people was a young woman who was expecting a child. The plantation overseer didn't let her rest for a moment, even as the birth grew near. He made her work harder and harder until one day she dropped down in the field. The overseer yelled at her to get up, but she just couldn't. The overseer cracked his whip across her back, but still she couldn't. Then an old man came to her side and helped her to her feet.

"Go," he said, "as you know how."

Slowly, beautiful wings unfolded from her shoulders. The woman rose up on her tiptoes. Soon her feet no longer touched the ground. Steadily, she climbed toward the sky.

The master and overseer ran after the young woman, trying to pull her back to land. But they couldn't. They turned instead on the old man, who only laughed at them. He laughed and laughed even as they lashed him with their whips.

"Don't you know who we are?" the old man asked. "We are the people who can fly!"

Then he gave a signal, and the rest of the slaves rose up and took flight. "Where they went, I do not know," the storyteller would say. Yet nothing the master did could bring them back to earth.

Music and Freedom

Music kept the rhythm of hope and freedom alive. It was as necessary to enslaved people as breathing air. Work songs eased the drudgery of hoeing, planting, and harvesting, while spirituals revived the spirits of tired souls. These songs were like shields that gave protection from the master's harsh words and the sting of his whip.

DRUMBEATS

Many masters forbade drumming. They thought drumming would remind their slaves of Africa and cause them to rise up and rebel. The masters also knew drumbeats could carry codes for escape—they didn't know the codes, but they knew enough to fear them.

Some slaves made beautiful drums, like those they remembered from Africa.

SONGS OF ESCAPE

Slaves also sang spirituals to send secret messages to each other that the slave owner wouldn't understand. The soft singing of songs like "Steal Away to Jesus" or "Go Down, Moses" signaled plans to escape. Moses was the biblical figure who led the Jewish people out of slavery in Egypt.

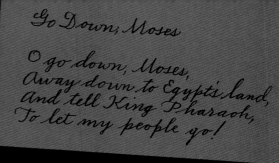

Go Down, Moses

O go down, Moses,
Away down to Egypt's land,
And tell King Pharaoh,
To let my people go!

Escaping slaves traveled north under the cover of darkness. Their main compass was the stars.

"The Drinking Gourd"

"Follow the drinking gourd . . . Left foot, right foot . . . traveling on, Follow the drinking gourd!" It sounded like a simple song, but its words were really a road map to freedom. The stars of the Big Dipper look like a hollowed-out drinking gourd. The cup points toward the north—and freedom.

The Mbanza Becomes a Banjo

A common musical instrument in Africa was a hollowed-out, long-necked gourd covered with an animal skin. This was called a *mbanza* (muh-BAHN-zah). The earliest slaves in America made simple mbanzas out of similar materials they found in America. During the 1800s, craftsmen began to make these musical instruments out of wood. They soon became what we now call banjos.

Lead On, Moses

One sweltering afternoon in about 1833, something extraordinary happened to a young slave named Harriet. She was working as usual, bent over a row of corn. Suddenly, a slave named Jim, who was working nearby, began to run across the field toward the woods. The overseer shouted, waved his bullwhip, and chased him. Harriet ran after both of them.

When Jim reached the crossroads, he ran into a small store. The overseer caught him and dragged him out the door. As he pulled out his whip, he told Harriet to grab Jim's legs and hold him down. But Harriet didn't move.

Jim soon wriggled free and ran. The overseer grabbed a weight from a scale on the porch and threw it at the runaway. But the weight missed Jim and hit Harriet, knocking her unconscious. For six months, Harriet lay nearly motionless in her mother's cabin. There was a deep wound in her forehead, which many believed had injured her brain. When Harriet finally came to, the other slaves believed her recovery was a miracle. To Harriet, it proved something she'd known for a long time: she was special—she was stronger and fiercer than other people, and she was without fear.

In 1849, Harriet decided to escape. She sought the help of a white Quaker woman, who told her how to follow the Underground Railroad. The Quaker gave Harriet a piece of paper, described a house many miles north of the plantation, and told Harriet to give the paper to the woman who came to the door.

Harriet had often heard about the Underground Railroad, but she'd thought it had to do with trains and tunnels. Now she realized it was something very different. The "conductor" who greeted her at the house gave Harriet food and a warm, dry bed. The next day she sent Harriet on to another "safe house."

The same thing happened day after day until she reached the free state of Pennsylvania.

Harriet was exhilarated by freedom. But having freedom just for herself wasn't enough. So Harriet became a conductor on the Underground Railroad. She saved so many black people from slavery that they began to call her "Moses," after the biblical figure who led the Jews to freedom. Soon masters and overseers heard about this Moses. They tacked up posters that read *"Wanted Dead or Alive—$40,000 REWARD!"* They thought the deep scar on her forehead would make her easy to identify. But they never found her.

It always happened the same way. First there was a rumor—*"the one called Moses is here, in the woods, by the river, near the slave quarters!"*—and the white men would search everywhere, even with dogs. The next morning, as the workday began, the master would realize that Moses had indeed been there. The strongest, hardest-working slaves had all vanished. They had followed Moses, and they were on their way to freedom.

Harriet Tubman was truly a legendary figure. Here she stands (far left) with six of the more than 300 slaves she led to freedom.

39

Soldiers, Spies, and Angels

Within months of the start of the Civil War, daring women and girls found ways to fight on the war front. Harriet Tubman sneaked into Confederate camps and freed captive slaves. Other women disguised themselves as men and enlisted as soldiers. Still others joined husbands and fathers on the front or worked as nurses—"angels of the battlefield." Some women and children even served as spies, endangering their lives to carry information and supplies across enemy lines!

THE COLONEL'S DAUGHTER
Lizzie Jones was 14 years old when she and her mother joined Lizzie's father on the front. Women and girls on the front helped with laundry and cooking, and nursed sick and wounded soldiers.

Lizzie wore this special "daughter of the regiment" uniform to ride at the head of regiment parades.

A pot used for making stew

WOMEN SOLDIERS
As many as 400 women disguised themselves as men and served without being discovered. Jennie Hodgers, above right, enlisted as "Private Albert Cashier" and served in the Union army throughout the war.

FEEDING THE FRONT
Most soldiers ate off wooden plates, but a few had fancy mess kits, like this one.

HARRIET TUBMAN

Harriet Tubman slipped behind Confederate lines, overheard secret plans, and then took the information to Union generals.

SPY DOLL

This doll, named Lucy Ann, helped smuggle medicine from the North to Rebel soldiers in the South. Her hollow head was filled with *quinine* (KWY-nine), which was used to treat malaria.

VOLUNTEER NURSES

Nurses gave medicine, changed bandages, and took care of wounded soldiers. If a soldier had an injured leg *amputated,* or cut off, a nurse might help him learn to walk with crutches.

Surgeon's tool kit

SPIES!

When the Union army approached Bull Run Creek in July 1861, the Confederates were waiting for them. That was because Mrs. Rose Greenbow had overheard the plan and sent a coded message to the Rebels in her daughter's silky curls!

ANGEL OF THE BATTLEFIELD

At the Battle of Antietam on September 17, 1862—the single bloodiest day of the Civil War— Clara Barton crossed the battle-field, bandaging and consoling wounded and dying soldiers. Then, as shells exploded around the army field hospital, she held the operating table steady so the surgeon could work. Her place, she said, was anywhere "between the bullet and the battlefield." She later founded the American Red Cross.

Nurses like Clara Barton helped army surgeons remove bullets from wounded soldiers.

41

Home Front: South

When southern women and children sent their husbands, fathers, and brothers off to war, few realized how much was about to change. Many white southern girls and women had been pampered and protected. They were not prepared for a life of independence, hard work, and hardship. They did not expect the slaves who had worked for them all their lives to leave. And they were not prepared for the battles that would be fought in their own backyards.

Bandages

OFF TO FIGHT
Most slaves got word of the Emancipation Proclamation from Union soldiers who shouted out the news as they marched past. When black men heard they were free, many left to fight for the Union. The women and children left behind had to work even harder than ever.

Women and girls made portable sewing kits for soldiers.

A Richmond, Virginia, sewing circle used 200 paper roses to make this flag.

LADIES' AID SOCIETIES
Women worked hard to support their soldiers on the front. They made bandages, shirts, and patriotic items such as flags to raise money to help sick and wounded soldiers.

Cannons and Caves

The Confederate city of Vicksburg, Mississippi, sat high on a bluff overlooking the mighty Mississippi River. It was an excellent lookout, and the Union army had decided to take it at any cost. In mid-May of 1863, Union soldiers began to attack.

As Union shells rained upon the streets and houses of Vicksburg, no one was safe. But the Confederate soldiers and citizens were not going to give up easily! To protect themselves, residents dug caves in the steep hillsides and bluffs above the river. There, they spent the night as the bombs fell around them. *"We ran to the small cave near the house,"* wrote one woman. *"I shall never forget . . . my utter hopelessness of ever seeing the morning light."* When morning finally came, many returned to their homes for the day. Slaves continued to do their masters' work, some starting the day by sweeping up shell fragments.

But the citizens of Vicksburg soon found they couldn't live a normal life, even by day. Lida Lord remembered, "Before sunset, a bombshell burst in the very center of that pretty dining room, blowing out the roof and one side, crushing the well-spread tea table like an eggshell, and making a great yawning hole in the floor into which disappeared supper, china, furniture, and the safe containing our entire stock of butter and eggs."

As the people of Vicksburg realized the battle would last more than just a few days, they dug more caves. Some had several rooms and were furnished with rugs, tables, and chairs. One woman reported being quite "comfortably fixed," with carpets on the floors and

A cannonball lands outside one of Vicksburg's caves.

Vicksburg residents dug hundreds of caves into steep hillsides to escape Union army bombs.

hung from the walls, and beds made from mattresses set on wooden planks. Still, as the days turned to weeks, hunger and sickness grew widespread. Finally, on July 4, 1863, the desperate Confederates raised a white flag of surrender. Soldiers and citizens came out of their trenches and caves, shocked to see what six weeks of shelling had done to their city—and the siege (seej) of Vicksburg ended.

That same day, word reached Vicksburg of another terrible Confederate defeat just one day earlier—in a battle fought on northern soil in faraway Gettysburg, Pennsylvania.

Home Front: North

The wartime lives of young girls and women in the North differed from state to state. Some were the daughters and wives of immigrant farmers in Minnesota or Wisconsin, and barely spoke English. To them, the war seemed far away—at least until their men left to fight. Others were the daughters of wealthy, educated men who never imagined life would be disrupted by war and death. Still others lived close enough to the front to see battles fought in their own backyards.

THEIR DUTY
Some men felt it was their duty to enlist, but many were *drafted*, or forced to enter the army. Some who could afford it paid $300 for a substitute to fight in their place.

Photo of brother

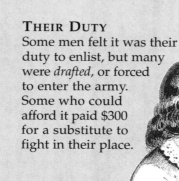

WHERE DID BROTHER GO?
Farm boys, whose lives seemed an endless round of dull chores, longed to join the army. Lying about one's age was common, and many 13- and 14-year-old boys marched into battle.

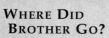

This 12-year-old drummer boy was wounded in the war.

LADIES' SEWING CIRCLES
Northern women made flags, wall hangings, and even potholders to raise money for Union and anti-slavery causes. These Philadelphia women gathered to sew a flag for a new Union regiment.

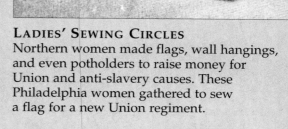

An anti-slavery potholder made in the 1860s by a woman in Illinois

44

Tillie Pierce of Gettysburg

"We had often heard that the Rebels were about to make a raid," wrote Tillie Pierce about the battle that took place in her hometown in 1863, when she was 15. *"But we had always found it a false alarm."* The Rebels did come at the very end of June 1863. A great number of them swarmed into Gettysburg, looking for Yankees. Tillie was at school at the Young Ladies Seminary when the words "The Rebels are coming!" echoed from every wall.

Tillie rushed home, burst through the door, and crouched below the parlor window to look out at the ragged Confederate soldiers. She heard her mother pleading with one of the Rebels to give back the horse he'd just stolen. But it was no use, and the soldier rode off on Tillie's favorite mare.

The next morning, Union troops arrived. *"A crowd of us girls were standing on the corner as these soldiers passed by,"* Tillie wrote. *"My sister started to sing the old war song 'Our Union Forever.'"* They sang chorus after chorus as the men marched up to nearby Cemetery Ridge—just across from the Confederate position at Seminary Ridge.

At ten o'clock, Tillie heard the first gunfire. Tillie's parents and older sister stayed in town to help take care of wounded soldiers, but they sent Tillie with a neighbor to the safety of a farmhouse just outside of town.

By the time Tillie reached the farm, it had been turned into a makeshift army hospital. Wagons filled with dead and wounded soldiers had already begun to arrive. Tillie went to work immediately, helping nurses and army surgeons by carrying buckets of water and bandages. *"The number of wounded . . . is indeed appalling,"* she wrote. *"They were laid in different parts of the house. The orchard and space around the buildings were covered with the shattered and dying. . . . It was terrible beyond description."*

From time to time, Tillie looked in the direction of the town of Gettysburg. All she could see was gray smoke. The smell and taste of gunpowder stung her nose and her throat. Could anyone in the town possibly survive?

Three days later, on July 3, the Union army defeated the Confederates—but at a terrible cost. Nearly 51,000 men were wounded or dead. Tillie rejoiced at the news that her own family was safe. Yet she—and the nation—despaired at the death and destruction that had changed the small town of Gettysburg forever.

Jubilation and Mourning

On April 9, 1865, the Civil War ended when Confederate General Robert E. Lee surrendered to Union General Ulysses S. Grant at Appomatox, Virginia. Riders on horseback galloped in all directions to spread the news, and most of America celebrated—especially the North. But less than one week later, a shattering event plunged the nation into despair once again.

SOUNDS OF VICTORY
Addy learned of the war's end when the crack of cannons woke her and her parents. Throughout the North, church bells pealed and firecrackers popped. People rushed to the streets to cheer and sing patriotic songs.

From the book Happy Birthday, Addy!

COMING HOME
With the war over, soldiers hurried home to their loved ones. More than 185,000 black soldiers fought in the Union army. Nearly one-quarter of them died.

PRESIDENT OF THE UNION
The long years of war had left President Lincoln's face lined and his hair gray. He told a friend, "Sometimes I think I'm the tiredest man on earth." This photograph was taken on April 10, 1865, one day after the war ended.

URRENDER OF GEN. LEE!

The Year of Jubilee has come! Let all the People Rejoice!"

200 GUNS WILL BE FIRED

On the Campus Martius,

AT 3 O'CLOCK TO-DAY, APRIL 10,

To Celebrate the Victories of our Armies.

Every Man, Woman and Child is hereby ordered to be on hand prepared to Sing and Rejoice. The crowd are expected to join in singing Patriotic Songs. PLACES OF BUSINESS MUST BE CLOSED AT 2 O'CLOCK.

d his noble Army.   *By Order of the People.*

A SINGLE SHOT

On Friday evening, April 14, the Lincolns went to the theater. As they watched the play, another actor, John Wilkes Booth, approached Mr. Lincoln from behind and shot him. The president died early the next morning. Sadness covered the country like a shroud.

The president's box at Ford's Theater

The president's oldest son, Robert Todd Lincoln, mourning the death of his father

TRAIN OF SORROW

President Lincoln's coffin was put on a train bound for his home in Springfield, Illinois. The funeral train followed the same route that Lincoln had taken to Washington as the newly elected president just four years earlier. At every station along the way, bells tolled, guns saluted, and cannons rumbled.

JOURNEY'S END

Seven million people had paid their respects to President Lincoln by the end of the journey. In Springfield, a horse-drawn funeral hearse took the coffin slowly down the streets of Lincoln's hometown. *We must now get along without him*, the people said. *But how?*

Freedom to Be a Family

After the war, freedmen returned to the plantations where they'd last seen their family members. "*Men are taking their wives and children, families which had been for a long time broken up are united, and oh! such happiness,*" wrote one Union officer to his wife. But sometimes a former owner tried to prevent a family from reuniting. "The mistress refused," remembered one woman, "and threatened to set the dogs on my mother if she did not at once leave the place." So her mother left and returned after dark, when she stole her own children away.

REUNION!
"They had a passion for getting together," said one observer, "Every mother's son seemed to be in search of his mother; every mother in search of her children."

WEDDING BELLS
Couples who had been married hastily during slavery wanted to be married "by the book." Marrying away from the master's watchful eye was a sign of true freedom.

FAMILY RECORDS
Black families in the South were free for the first time to write down and keep their family histories. Under slavery, they could have been punished for such records.

A bride's hair wreath made of orange blossoms

Born
Married
Died

Born
Married
Died

Born
Married
Died

Born
Married
Died

Born
Married
Died

BEFO

Southern black families who could afford it had family photos taken.

PICTURE PERFECT?
Images of reunited families printed on pamphlets and family records often showed an *idealized*, or imagined, view of what family life would be like for black Americans after the war.

FAMILY RECORD

I have a mother somewhere in the world, I know not where.
Reverend E. W. Johnson

WAR · AND · SINCE · THE · WAR.

THE REAL PICTURE
Unfortunately, some former slaves never found their families. Even for those who did, earning a living and building a new life was a struggle—despite the warmth of family love.

Jubilee!

Many African Americans celebrated Emancipation Day on January 1, the anniversary of Abraham Lincoln's Emancipation Proclamation in 1863. That day is also called *Jubilee*, which means a special time of rejoicing. Jubilee was the time to celebrate freedom with family and friends. Often Jubilee began much as Addy's did, with a reading of the Emancipation Proclamation at a late-night church service on New Year's Eve. On New Year's Day the Jubilee celebration continued as families shared food and sang special Jubilee songs.

Eventually, Jubilee became part of a summer celebration as well. Enslaved people in Texas didn't get word of the Proclamation until June 19, 1865. Black people there started having "Juneteenth" gatherings to celebrate their freedom.

From the book *Changes for Addy*

FREEDMEN'S SCHOOLS
By the end of the war, freedmen's schools had been started all across the South in churches, in barns, and even under trees. Teachers from the North watched with pride as whole families came to school together.

Freedom to Learn

Newly freed African Americans knew that education was important in building the future. Because learning to read and write had been illegal under slavery, very few people had even these basic skills. During the war, a few schools for blacks had been started in the South, mostly by teachers from the North. But after the war ended, churches, charities, and the government's Freedmen's Bureau helped bring education to young and old alike.

"TO TEACH MY PEOPLE"
Fanny Jackson Coppin became principal of Philadelphia's Institute for Colored Youth in 1869—the first black principal in America. She sent many I.C.Y. graduates to teach in the South.

The Union ABC used patriotic figures, colors, and rhymes to help students learn to read.

EAGER TO LEARN
School buildings for black students were often crumbling and had few supplies. Very young teachers—some only 16 years old—struggled with large classes. Still, the hunger to learn kept students coming back.

Students reciting at a school for newly freed people

A soldier reads aloud to his elderly grandparents.

Inkwell and pens from the 1860s

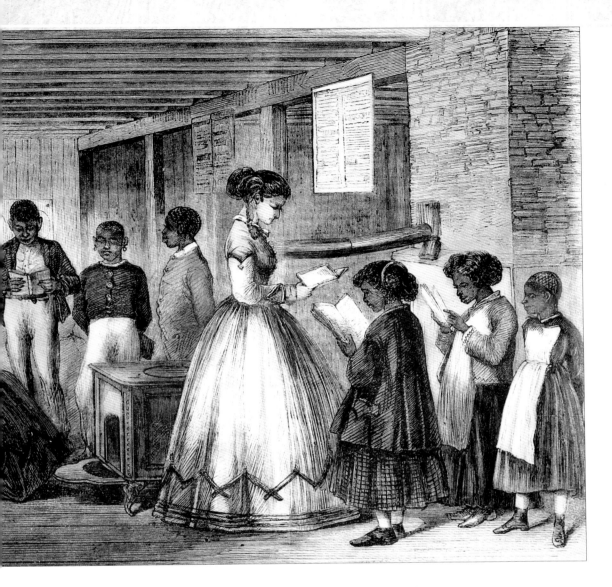

The Fisk Jubilee Singers

Fisk University in Nashville, Tennessee, was opened as a college for black students in 1866. But in 1870, the university's funds were cut. It looked as if Fisk would have to close its doors.

Then music teacher George White had an idea. The students at Fisk loved to gather and sing the spirituals they'd learned as children. George White decided to organize these students into a concert choir. In 1871, the Jubilee Singers—named in honor of the Emancipation Proclamation—started touring to raise money for the school. Most white Northerners had never heard gospel music and spirituals and were stunned by their beauty. They flocked to concert halls and gave standing ovations.

The Fisk Jubilee Singers performed for Queen Victoria in England. In Washington they sang for two presidents—even though they weren't allowed as guests at any hotel in the entire city.

In seven years of touring, they raised $150,000, enough money to buy the university's land and build its first permanent building—Jubilee Hall.

Some students learned to count using an abacus. They were encouraged to count the beads instead of their fingers.

A New South

After the war ended, southern cities like Richmond and Atlanta were in shambles from shelling and fires, and many plantations and farms were ruined or abandoned. The government in Washington poured money into the *Reconstruction,* or the rebuilding of the South. It was a hopeful time, as families reunited and people returned to their homes and businesses. Blacks in the South began to enjoy new freedoms. But soon, many white Southerners grew angry and resentful of those freedoms. They did everything they could to keep black people "in their place."

CARPETBAGGERS
Many Northerners packed their bags and went south to help with the rebuilding. Some were given the negative nickname *carpetbaggers* because they made hasty changes and repairs and then packed their carpetbags and moved on to make more money elsewhere.

Much of the city of Richmond, Virginia, was destroyed during the war.

BLACK CODES
White Southerners—many of them former slave owners—passed laws called *Black Codes* to limit the freedom of black people. Laws stated that blacks could be fined or imprisoned for not working for a white person or for forming a black church without police permission.

VOTING FOR THE FIRST TIME
After the war, Congress *amended,* or changed, the Constitution to give black men the right to vote and run for office. But no women, black or white, would be given those same rights for another fifty years.

LAWMAKERS
During the Reconstruction, 16 African American men were elected to Congress, and more than 600 became state representatives throughout the South. Hiram R. Revels, elected to the U.S. Senate from Mississippi, was America's first black senator.

KKK ROBES
In late 1865, an ex–Confederate general formed the Ku Klux Klan. This secret society hated both black people and the white people who supported them. Klan members dressed in white robes with hoods over their faces. They came to people's homes in the middle of the night to harrass or even murder them.

Moving On

Black Codes and increasing violence toward blacks kept many black people living in poverty and fear. A Mississippi teacher wrote, *"We are hardworking people but cannot reap the benefit of our labor."* In 1877, when the last government troops left the South, an *exodus*—or mass journey—out of the South began. Many black families left to make a fresh start in a new place—out west, up north, or anywhere they could be free of the South.

Posters advertised inexpensive land out west. Within six months, 6,000 southern blacks left for Kansas.

Ho for Kansas!

Brethren, Friends, & Fellow Citizens:
I feel thankful to inform you that the
REAL ESTATE
AND
Homestead Association,
Will Leave Here the
15th of April, 1878,
In pursuit of Homes in the Southwestern Lands of America, at Transportation Rates, cheaper than ever was known before.

For full information inquire of
Benj. Singleton, better known as old Pap,
NO. 5 NORTH FRONT STREET.

Beware of Speculators and Adventurers, as it is a dangerous thing to fall in their hands.

Nashville, Tenn., March 18, 1878.

WESTWARD BOUND
All along the southern part of the Mississippi River, families camped on the banks, waiting for steamboats to take them west.

EXODUSTERS

Blacks who left the South and settled on the flat and dusty plains of Kansas were called "Exodusters." The name refers to the biblical story of the Jews' exodus from slavery in Egypt. One woman remembered the sod houses as "not at all inviting, and I began to cry." Yet the Exodusters built more sod homes, planted wheat, and made Kansas their home.

A POWERFUL STATEMENT

Some people thought blacks should stay and fight for their rights. But others, like the reformer Sojourner Truth, believed the exodus was the most powerful statement black people could make against the cruelties of the South.

Riding the Range

Nat Love was a former slave who left Tennessee for a life of adventure in the Wild West. Nat decided to become a cowboy and got a job riding the trail in Texas. He worked as a *brand reader*, someone who branded calves and kept track of the herd on the trail.

Nat Love's skills as a rider and roper were legendary. After he won every event in an 1876 rodeo contest in Deadwood, South Dakota, the townspeople honored him by giving him the nickname "Deadwood Dick."

Later that same year, Nat was taken prisoner and then adopted by a tribe of Indians. He learned new skills from the Indians, but he wanted to return to his life as a cowboy. Under the cover of night, Nat slipped away on a fast Indian pony and went back to life on the trail.

When the West started filling up with towns and cities that were connected by the railroad, Nat Love decided it was time to trade the trail for rails. In 1890, he took a job with the railroad and left the cowboy life behind.

Nat Love wrote about his amazing life in **The Life and Adventures of Nat Love.**

Mending the Nation Piece by Piece

I n the years after the Civil War, African American reformers, writers, artists, and inventors continued the struggle to improve the lives of black people. Through efforts large and small, they used their courage and energy to mend the nation. This quilt, created in 1991 by artist Faith Ringgold, celebrates some of the women who have worked for freedom, justice, and the advancement of African Americans from Addy's time until today. They are shown piecing together a quilt, just as each of them worked to "make this world piece up right."

This quilt was made by an enslaved woman in 1839.

SOJOURNER TRUTH
Born a slave, Isabella Baumfree took the name Sojourner Truth after she was freed. She traveled the country to speak the truth about slavery and the rights of women.

A TRADITION OF QUILTING
West Africans brought their quilting traditions to America. Slaves had few possessions, but took pride in the beautiful quilts they created from scraps.

HARRIET TUBMAN
Harriet's work didn't stop with the end of slavery. She helped start black schools and worked for the rights of women. When she died at age 92, flags in New York City were lowered to half-mast.

IDA B. WELLS
Ida B. Wells was a teacher who lost her job because she spoke out about the bad conditions of black schools. She became known in the 1890s for writing about violence against blacks.

MADAM C. J. WALKER
In the early 1900s, Madam Walker's hair care products made her the first black American woman to become a millionaire. Her business created thousands of jobs for black people.

The sunflowers in this quilt were inspired by a painting by artist Vincent Van Gogh, who is shown in the corner of the quilt.

FANNIE LOU HAMER
Fannie Lou Hamer faced brutal beatings, police dogs, and jail time, but she continued her work of getting black voters to the polls during the 1960s.

MARY MCLEOD BETHUNE
Mary McLeod Bethune started a girls' school that became an important black college in the 1920s. She was also an adviser to two presidents on the needs of black people.

ELLA BAKER
Ella Baker realized that poor housing was a serious problem for blacks. Starting in the 1930s, she organized thousands of black people to improve their living conditions.

ROSA PARKS
In 1955, Rosa Parks was arrested because she sat in a bus seat reserved for white people and refused to move. Her brave act led to the end of segregation on Montgomery, Alabama, city buses.

A Peek into the Future

From the book *Changes for Addy*

"It's all right, child," Auntie Lula said. "Uncle Solomon died a free man. He did what he set out to do."

—Changes for Addy

When Addy's family was finally reunited after the war, the joy of finding Auntie Lula and Esther was mixed with sadness over the death of Uncle Solomon. Still, Addy and her family faced the future with hope.

At the end of the war, Congress amended the Constitution to end slavery and to give citizenship to black Americans. Black men like Poppa could vote in elections, and they did so in large numbers.

Addy probably read aloud newspaper articles to her family about the Black Codes in the South, or heard about them firsthand from black people who came to the North during the exodus. She and her family might have heard speeches by Ida B. Wells and other leaders who spoke out against the segregation and violence that kept blacks from enjoying the same freedoms as whites.

The words of these leaders may have inspired Addy to work even harder to reach her dream of becoming a teacher. Perhaps one day she did graduate from Philadelphia's Institute for Colored Youth. After graduation, she might have gone back to the South to teach.

Institute for Colored Youth

Addy probably would have married and had children of her own. Perhaps they fought for equality for blacks, or for votes for women. Her grandchildren and great-grandchildren might have become leaders in the fight for rights that continues even today, as men and women of all races work for justice in America.